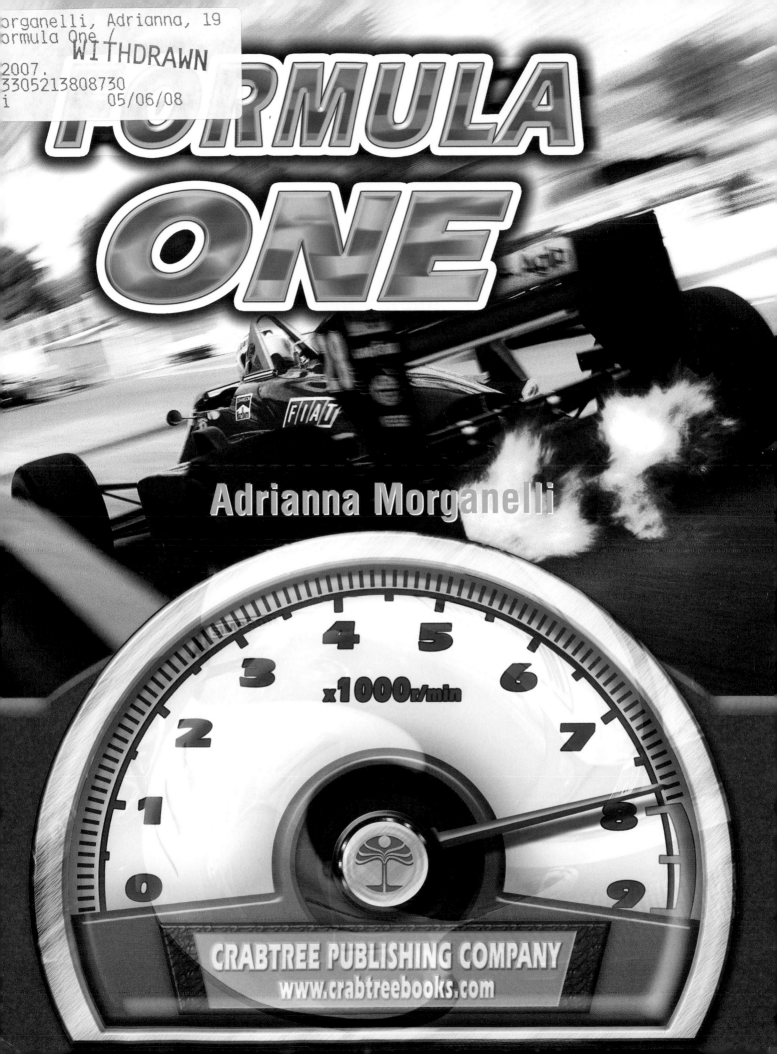

FORMULA ONE

Adrianna Morganelli

x1000r/min

CRABTREE PUBLISHING COMPANY
www.crabtreebooks.com

Crabtree Publishing Company

www.crabtreebooks.com

For my dad, Nick, and his love for Formula One.

Coordinating editor: Ellen Rodger
Series and project editor: Rachel Eagen
Editors: Carrie Gleason, L. Michelle Nielsen
Design and production coordinator: Rosie Gowsell
Production assistance: Samara Parent
Art direction: Rob MacGregor
Scanning technician: Arlene Arch-Wilson
Photo research: Allison Napier

Consultant: Norm Mort, automotive historian and journalist

Photo Credits: The Art Archive/Royal Automobile Club London/NB Design: p. 5 (bottom); The Art Archive/Domenica del Corriere/Dagli Orti: p. 8 (top); AP/Wide World Photos: pp. 10-11, p. 14, p. 15 (top), p. 22 (top); Bettmann/Corbis: p. 29 (bottom); Gero Breloer/epa/Corbis: p. 29 (top); Eric Gaillard/Reuters/Corbis: p. 31 (top); Eva-Lotta

Jansson/Corbis: p. 21; Kim Ludbrook/epa/Corbis: p. 30 (bottom); Schlegelmilch/Corbis: cover, p. 1, p. 4, p. 5 (top), p. 8 (bottom), p. 9, p. 11, p. 12 (both), p. 13 (bottom right), p. 15 (bottom), p. 16, p. 17, p. 18, p. 19 (both), p. 20, p. 22 (bottom), p. 23 (top), p. 24 (both), p. 25, p. 26 (both), p. 27 (both), p. 28 (both), p. 29 (middle), p. 30 (top), p. 31 (middle and bottom); Jad Sherif/World Racing Images/Corbis: p. 13 (bottom left); SSPL/The Image Works: p. 6; Collection Roger-Viollet/The Image Works: p. 7 (both); Maximilian Stock Ltd./Photo Researchers, Inc.: p. 13 (top); Courtesy of Simpson Performance Products: p. 23 (all on bottom). Other images from stock CD.

Cover: Formula One driver Michael Schumacher, racing for Ferrari, leads the pack at the Canadian Grand Prix.

Title page: A Formula One car shoots down the track.

Library and Archives Canada Cataloguing in Publication

Morganelli, Adrianna, 1979-
   Formula One / Adrianna Morganelli.

(Automania!)
Includes index.
ISBN-13: 978-0-7787-3009-5 (bound)
ISBN-10: 0-7787-3009-3 (bound)
ISBN-13: 978-0-7787-3031-6 (pbk.)
ISBN-10: 0-7787-3031-X (pbk.)
   1. Formula One automobiles--Juvenile literature. 2. Grand Prix racing--Juvenile literature. I. Title. II. Series.

GV1029.13.M67 2006   j796.72   C2006-902460-X

Library of Congress Cataloging-in-Publication Data

Morganelli, Adrianna, 1979-
   Formula One / written by Adrianna Morganelli.
     p. cm. -- (Automania!)
Includes index.
ISBN-13: 978-0-7787-3009-5 (rlb)
ISBN-10: 0-7787-3009-3 (rlb)
ISBN-13: 978-0-7787-3031-6 (pb)
ISBN-10: 0-7787-3031-X (pb)
   1. Formula One automobiles--Juvenile literature. I. Title. II. Series.

TL236.M65 2006
   796.72--dc22

                            2006014362

Crabtree Publishing Company

www.crabtreebooks.com   1-800-387-7650

Published in Canada
Crabtree Publishing
616 Welland Ave.
St. Catharines, ON
L2M 5V6

Published in the United States
Crabtree Publishing
PMB16A
350 Fifth Ave., Suite 3308
New York, NY 10118

Published in the United Kingdom
Crabtree Publishing
White Cross Mills
High Town, Lancaster
LA1 4XS

Published in Australia
Crabtree Publishing
386 Mt. Alexander Rd.
Ascot Vale (Melbourne)
VIC 3032

Contents

Start Your Engines!

Formula One racing is the most competitive and technologically advanced motor racing championship in the world. The races, called Grand Prix, take place on specially designed circuits, or tracks, where race teams, drivers, and constructors battle for the glory of winning a World Championship.

A Global Sport

Lured by the world's most skilled drivers and fastest cars, more than 120,000 spectators from around the world attend each Formula One race. Grand Prix races take place on tracks in many different countries around the world. The drivers are of all nationalities and the cars and engines are designed and manufactured worldwide.

A pack of Formula One cars speed down the track on race day.

Formula One Cars

Formula One cars are called "formula" because they are designed according to strict specifications that are outlined in the rule book. "One" means that the cars are the best in formula racing. The cars are open-wheeled, meaning the wheels are located outside of the cars' bodies. The cars are extremely lightweight, and have **cockpits** that seat only the drivers. Formula One race cars are the fastest in racing, reaching speeds of up to 200 miles per hour (322 kilometers per hour).

The F.I.A.

A motor sport organization called the Fédération Internationale de l'Automobile (F.I.A.) controls Formula One racing. Many different motoring clubs came together to form the organization in 1904, and it officially became known as the F.I.A. in 1947. The F.I.A. makes the rule book, which includes technical and sporting regulations. Included in the sporting regulations is the points system, which is used to determine the winners of the driver and the constructor World Championships.

(above) Over 120,000 spectators crowd into stadiums to watch Formula One races, while another 300 million watch on TV.

(right) Race day programs from early British Grand Prix races at Donington Park, in England.

Early Races

In the late 1800s and early 1900s, car manufacturers tested and displayed their new car models at racing circuits that ran from one city to another. Grand Prix racing quickly grew from these simple races to a highly competitive sport that tested the endurance of the car and driver.

Gordon Bennett Cup

In 1900, James Gordon Bennett Jr., an American businessman living in France, established an **annual** car racing competition called the Gordon Bennett Cup. Drivers from all over Europe and the United States raced in the competition. French race car driver Fernand Charron won the first Gordon Bennett Cup, which ran on public roads between the cities of Paris and Lyon, in France. He raced in a car built by a French auto company called Panhard-Levassor.

A Grand Idea

Each country was allowed to enter only three cars in the Gordon Bennett Cup. France was considered the top car producer at the time, and French constructors wanted to enter more of their cars into the races to ensure a French win. In 1906, the French decided to create their own racing competition called the Grand Prix, which means "Grand Prize" in French. Car **manufacturers** were allowed to enter as many race cars as they wished into Grand Prix races.

Camille Jenatzy races to the finish line at the Gordon Bennett Cup race of 1903, held in Athy, Ireland. Jenatzy completed the 327-mile (526-kilometer) race in six hours and 39 minutes.

The Gordon Bennett Cup trophy featured two angelic figures riding in a car similar to ones raced at the competition. The races took place from 1900 until 1905.

Grand Prix Races Catch On

The first Grand Prix race was held in Le Mans, France, in 1906. Thirty-four cars competed in this race, which represented 13 different car manufacturers. The race was held over two days, and ran on a triangular circuit of closed public roads in the countryside called Circuit de la Sarthe. Drivers completed six laps of the course on both days, each lap covering 65 miles (105 kilometers). This distance took drivers about six hours to complete. It was not long before other countries, such as Italy, Belgium, and Spain, created their own Grand Prix races. The racing rules varied in each country, but strict limitations were placed on the weight of the vehicles and the size of their engines. This was done so that some cars would not have advantages over others, and to make the competition as fair as possible.

In the early days of Grand Prix racing, the driver and a mechanic rode in each car. They were the only people who were allowed to work on the car during the race. By the early 1920s, Grand Prix cars were built to seat only the driver.

Creating a Formula

Grand Prix racing quickly became popular in Europe, but Grand Prix races were different in every country. In 1925, the first World Championship was awarded. Top drivers and car manufacturers across the various Grand Prix series competed for the title.

World Championship

The first World Championship awarded the constructor who made the best and most reliable race car. Points were given to the winning cars over four different races, and the constructor with the vehicle with the most points at the end of the season was declared the winner. In 1950, the F.I.A. organized the first World Championship for drivers. Points were awarded to the winning drivers over five different Grand Prix races. Italian race car driver Giuseppe Farina became the first World Champion on May 13, 1950, at the Silverstone circuit in Britain.

Teaming Up

When Grand Prix racing first started, car manufacturers built their cars from parts that they made themselves, including the engines, **gearboxes**, and frames. In the 1950s, car manufacturers began buying automotive parts from specialized factories and engine specialists. These partnerships allowed racing teams to develop faster and more powerful cars. Some of these first racing teams included Cooper-Bristol, Brabham-BRM, and Lotus-Climax.

(above) Italian driver Antonio Ascari winning a Grand Prix race in 1925. He died later that year in a car crash.

(below) Australian driver Jack Brabham takes the lead at the Monaco Grand Prix. He formed his own racing team in 1962.

Mega Points

In today's Formula One races, the first eight drivers to cross the finish line are awarded points, which are counted toward the World Championship title. Constructors are awarded a combination of their drivers' points. For example, if one driver on a team scores 4 points, and the other driver on the same team scores 6 points, the constructor is awarded 10 points for the race. These points are counted toward the World Constructors' Championship.

Place	Points
1st	10
2nd	8
3rd	6
4th	5
5th	4
6th	3
7th	2
8th	1

The Look of Speed

Until the late 1960s, Formula One cars were painted in their national colors. Italy was represented by red, France by blue, Britain by green, Germany by white, and Belgium by yellow. In 1968, Colin Chapman, the team boss of the British racing team Lotus, wrote to 100 different British companies and asked for their **sponsorship**. A cigarette company called Gold Leaf agreed to fund the team. That season, Lotus race cars were painted in Gold Leaf colors, which were red, white, and gold. Today, Formula One cars are covered with the **logos** of their sponsors.

(above) Formula One cars bear advertising from many different sponsors. Corporations are eager to support successful drivers because it helps them promote their products or services. Sponsors help carry the high costs of running a team and maintaining the cars.

All Revved Up

Formula One cars are extremely lightweight, powerful, and fast. The superior design and assembly of the cars help drivers brake, accelerate, and handle corners with ease.

Wings

The term aerodynamics describes the way in which air flows around, beneath, and over the surface of a car. Each Formula One team has an aerodynamic designer, whose main jobs are to help the cars create more downforce, and to minimize the amount of air resistance, or **drag,** that slows down the cars. Downforce is the pressure pushing down on the car caused by air passing over it during a race. Wings at the front and rear of the cars create downforce, or help push the cars to the ground. The wings help stabilize the car, as the air flowing beneath it lifts the car up. Barge boards are pieces of metal that are attached to the sides of the cars. They separate the air and minimize **turbulence,** allowing the cars to race even faster.

Tub and Chassis

The main body of a Formula One car is called the "tub," and it is where the driver sits. The tub is attached to the chassis. The chassis is the basic frame of the car, including the steering, **suspension**, engine, and **drivetrain**. The chassis is made from a lightweight material called **carbon fiber**, and weighs about 66 pounds (30 kilograms). It must be strong enough to withstand more than 4,409 pounds (2,000 kilograms) of downforce.

Engine

Formula One engines burn a mixture of air and gasoline within **cylinders**. A piston **compresses** the mixture inside each cylinder, which is **ignited** by a device called a spark plug. This process produces energy to power the car. In 2006, the F.I.A. ruled that all Formula One engines must have eight cylinders. Previously, ten-cylinder engines were standard. The rule slows down the cars and helps keep drivers safer.

Transmission

The transmission is the system of **gears** and other parts that work to send power from the engine to the wheels. Low gears are used for traveling at slower speeds around tight corners, while high gears are used for racing at top speeds on straight stretches. Formula One cars have semi-automatic transmissions, which means that the drivers change gears using paddles on the back of the steering wheel. This allows drivers to keep both hands on the steering wheel at all times, giving them more control.

Inside the Cockpit

The cockpit is made to balance the car's **center of gravity**. The driver's seat is molded to fit the driver's body. A brake pedal is on the left side of the cockpit, and an accelerator pedal, which controls the flow of fuel to the engine, is on the right. The steering wheel has many controls for various functions, such as communicating with the pit crew and the engineers, and changing the car's handling characteristics.

(below) The steering wheel of a Formula One car has many different functions to help the driver control the car, including a speed limiter for slowing down in the pit lane, a button to adjust the fuel-air mixture in the engine, and a radio for communicating with teammates.

(below) Ralf Schumacher slides into the cockpit of his car before the Japanese Grand Prix. The driver's seat is specially designed to fit snugly around the driver's body to prevent the driver from moving around and bruising on the track.

Tires

The F.I.A. limits the width and tread groove of the tires on the wheels of Formula One cars. The back tires are wider than the front tires because most of the mechanical parts of the car are located at the rear, placing more weight there. The tires' grip on the track is determined by their compound, or the chemicals that make up the materials that the tires are made from. Tire manufacturers create different compounds for different tracks based on track design and surface.

(below) From the 1960s to 1998, Formula One cars raced with slick tires, or tires that did not have treads. The F.I.A. has made grooved tires mandatory so that drivers can maintain better control of their cars and increase safety.

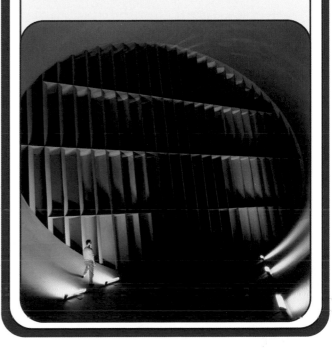

Wind Tunnel

Formula One teams use wind tunnels to test the aerodynamics of their cars. Wind machines duplicate conditions on a track. Race teams can then make changes to improve speed.

(below) Wings help keep cars stable on the track. A camera is mounted above the wings of this car so the team can have an up-close view of how their car is performing on the track.

Making the Grid

Grand Prix weekends involve much more than showing up for the race. Race teams attend practice sessions and qualifying rounds before they arrive at the starting line. They must also meet the strict technical regulations that are set up in the rule book, and pass several pre-race checks from watchful scrutineers.

Quest for the Pole

The starting grid is the arrangment of cars at the starting line. Qualifying rounds determine the position that each car will take on the grid. There are 11 teams, each represented by two drivers on race day. This means that there are 22 cars on the starting grid. During the first qualifying round, the cars are timed as they speed around one lap of the track as fast as possible. The six slowest cars are given positions 17 to 22 on the grid. During the second qualifying round, the six slowest cars are assigned positions 11 to 16. The remaining 10 cars are timed in a third qualifying round. The fastest car is awarded the first position on the grid, which is called pole position.

(below) An official checks a Ferrari race car and talks to members of the team at the Bahrain International Circuit at the Bahrain Grand Prix.

And the Winner is...

A black-and-white checkered flag is waved when the first race car crosses the finish line. The winner then completes one more lap of the track, called the victory lap. During this lap, **race marshals** along the sides of the track wave flags at the driver to offer their congratulations. The winning car is then inspected for violations to the regulations. After being weighed, the winner and the second and third place drivers climb a **podium**, where they are awarded with trophies and champagne. The winner then attends television interviews and a **press conference** before joining the racing team to celebrate their victory.

Michael Schumacher salutes his fans in triumph as he crosses the finish line of the French Grand Prix at Magny-Cours, France.

Penalties

Drivers are penalized for breaking rules, such as jumping the start, unfairly blocking or forcing another driver off the track, speeding in the pit lane, or causing an avoidable accident. A drive-through penalty forces a driver to enter and drive through the pits at the area's speed limit before rejoining the race. The ten-second penalty, or the stop-and-go penalty, requires the driver to enter the pits and stop for ten seconds before rejoining the race. The worst penalty is when a driver must drop ten grid positions at the next Grand Prix. This means that if the driver had qualified to start the race at the pole position, the driver must start the race from the eleventh position instead.

The Flags

During Grand Prix races, marshals use flags to communicate with the drivers. Below is a list of some of the flags and their meanings.

Yellow - Danger; slow down
Black - Go to the pits
Blue - A car is trying to pass
Red - Stop; unsafe track
White - Slow car on the track
Yellow with red stripes - Oil on the track
Checkered - Winner has crossed the finish line

Racing Circuits

Formula One races are not held on oval tracks as in other motor sport races, such as stock car races. The races take place on different types of circuits. Each circuit presents different challenges to the teams and drivers.

Street Tracks

Street tracks are closed sections of narrow and winding public roads, which are open to traffic on non-race days. The width of the track makes it very difficult for cars to pass other cars. For this reason, it is important that drivers get a good grid position during the qualifying rounds.

(above) The German Grand Prix is held on a high-speed circuit called Hockenheimring. It is one of the fastest Formula One circuits.

High-speed Tracks

High-speed tracks have few corners, with long, straight stretches for the cars to reach top speeds. These stretches are called straights. On high-speed tracks, Formula One teams set up their cars to achieve minimum downforce to make them as fast as possible while driving the straights. Long straights are often broken up by chicanes, or series of corners on the track, to slow down the cars and to help the drivers maintain control. Most Formula One races are held on medium-speed tracks.

Medium-speed Tracks

Medium-speed tracks are a combination of straight stretches and tight corners. They are slower than high-speed tracks because they have several hairpin turns, or sharp corners. Formula One cars are equipped with extra aerodynamic wings and devices to increase downforce and maintain grip on medium-speed tracks.

(above) The Grand Prix of San Marino is held on the Autodromo Enzo e Dino Ferrari circuit. The track is a combination of medium- to high-speed corners, with long, high-speed straights.

(right) The Monaco Grand Prix in Monte Carlo is held on the most famous street track in Formula One racing. The race covers 78 laps, each covering 2.1 miles (3.3 kilometers).

Grand Prix Races

There are 18 Grand Prix races in the Formula One season, which runs from March to October. Huge crowds of fans fill the stadiums, and millions more watch the races from home on television.

The U.S. Grand Prix

The United States Grand Prix is held on the Indianapolis Motor Speedway, one of the world's oldest functioning tracks. The track was originally built from crushed stones and tar when it was made in 1908, but was later replaced with bricks, earning its nickname "The Brickyard." The track was finally surfaced with asphalt in the early 1960s. The U.S. Grand Prix includes 73 laps, each a distance of 2.6 miles (four kilometers).

Rubens Barrichello won the 2002 U.S. Grand Prix. A strip of bricks at the finish line is a tribute to the original Brickyard.

The British Grand Prix

The Silverstone Circuit in England is a former airdrome, or military base. The facility was made into a racing circuit after World War II. One of the most exciting Grand Prix races at Silverstone happened in 1987, when Brazilian driver Nelson Piquet and British driver Nigel Mansell battled each other to the finish line. Mansell was gaining on Piquet's lead when his car was thrown off balance by damaged front tires. Mansell was forced to the pits for new tires, and re-entered the race 30 seconds behind Piquet, with 30 laps to go. Two laps from the finish, Mansell blocked Piquet and won the race. Mansell's car ran out of fuel during the victory lap.

European Grand Prix

The European Grand Prix is held on the Nürburgring Circuit in Nürburgring, Germany. The circuit was originally a 14-mile (22.5-kilometer) track with 172 corners, but it was shut down due to unsafe conditions after Viennese driver Niki Lauda crashed his Ferrari at the 1976 European Grand Prix. The track was completely changed and reopened for races in 1984. One of the most memorable European Grand Prix races took place in 1993. The track was wet and slippery due to heavy rain. During the first lap of the race, Brazilian driver Ayrton Senna, racing for McLaren, passed Ferrari's Michael Schumacher and headed toward a fast downhill section of the circuit. All of the drivers drove through this section in single file, not wanting to risk sliding off-course in the wet conditions. Senna pulled out to the right and passed all of the cars ahead of him. Senna's dangerous first lap is considered by many fans to be the best first lap in Formula One history.

The British Grand Prix is held at the Silverstone track in England. Drivers must complete 60 laps, each covering 3.2 miles (5.1 kilometers).

Staying Safe

During the early days of Formula One racing, drivers wore cotton clothing and leather safety helmets, and the cars were a very basic design. Technological advances in race car design, safety procedures on race circuits, and protective clothing have helped make the sport much safer.

Designed for Safety

Formula One race cars are made from strong materials, have special casings for the fuel tanks, or cells, as well as built-in fire extinguishers for the engines. All of these features improve the safety of the driver. Drivers are strapped firmly into the cockpits with five-point seat belts, which have one strap that goes over each shoulder, one strap that comes up between the drivers' legs, and one that comes from either side of the car and over the drivers' laps. Drivers can remove the steering wheels quickly if they need to exit their cars.

(top right) Drivers wear long underwear made of a fire-resistant material called Nomex. This protects them if their cars catch fire.

(right) Rollover hoops are strong metal bars in front of and behind the cockpit to protect drivers from being crushed if their cars flip over.

Headgear

Drivers wear fireproof head coverings called balaclavas under their custom-made safety helmets. They also wear earplugs to protect their hearing from the loud roar of the engines. Helmets have visors made from strong materials to protect the drivers' eyes from dust and debris. Many visors are tinted to keep the sun out of the drivers' eyes. The cockpit of a Formula One car gets extremely hot during a race. To guard drivers against **dehydration**, helmets are equipped with a mouthpiece and thin tube for drivers to drink fluids from during the race.

(above) Nigel Mansell shown in a balaclava before a race.

(below) Drivers must wear Head and Neck Support systems, or HANS, which are collars that attach onto their helmets. This prevents their heads from snapping forward or sideways in an accident.

Safety Clothing

All pieces of clothing that Formula One drivers wear are made of a fire-resistant material called Nomex. Drivers wear long underwear, T-shirts, and socks made from this material, as well as overalls, which zip up the front and cover their arms and legs. Drivers wear fire resistant gloves that have leather patches to help them grip the steering wheel and maintain better control of their cars. The boots that drivers are required to wear are made of a fire resistant rubber and have very thin soles so that they can feel the pedals through them.

The Race Team

There are from 600 to 900 people involved in a Formula One team. They all have different areas of expertise. Teams are organized into various departments, but everyone works toward the same goal on race day: WINNING!

Yes, Boss

The team boss usually builds the team, finds sponsors to fund it, and makes many important decisions, such as hiring the head mechanics and engineers. The team boss is also responsible for purchasing the latest technology for the team so they can continue to test and develop the best equipment, and build the best vehicles they can.

(below) Members of the Ferrari racing team cheer on their driver.

(above) Michael Schumacher celebrates a victory. Formula One drivers are skilled, talented people, but they would never make it to the winners' podium without their teammates.

Head Honchos

There are several people who report directly to the team boss. The chief of design works with a team of designers and engineers to develop the design for the race car. The chief of aerodynamics analyzes data collected from wind tunnel tests, and advises other personnel on how to modify the cars so that they can cut through the wind on the track and improve handling. The chief of research and development oversees a department that experiments with new materials and technology to improve the way their cars perform under different track and weather conditions.

In the Garage

Many team members are responsible for the manufacturing and maintenance of a Formula One race car. Mechanics and auto body specialists design various parts, such as the engine, transmission, and chassis. Teams of toolmakers, welders, machinists, and assemblers put the car together. Each driver works with a race engineer on the day of the race to determine the best set-up for the car. This involves making adjustments to the suspension, wings, and other parts of the car so that the drivers can maintain control and achieve the best speed on the track.

Pit Crew

A pit crew of up to 20 people service a car during a pit stop. The car is raised up on **jacks** so the crew can change all four tires. The pit crew refuels the car, then checks it and makes minor repairs. Other members of the pit crew clean the dirt, oil, and sweat off the driver's visor. Timing is crucial during a pit stop, as a few extra seconds can cost the team a race. Most pit stops take about 30 seconds.

(below) Members of the Renault pit crew stand back while their car races in for a pit stop.

Born to Race

Successful Formula One drivers are rewarded for their skill on the track with large sums of money, millions of fans, and endorsements. At every race, Formula One drivers risk severe injury, and even death, to achieve these rewards.

Having What it Takes

Formula One drivers are pushed to their limits during every Grand Prix. They must be physically fit and be able to withstand the intense heat inside the cockpit. They also must concentrate and keep aware of pit signals, warning flags, their opponents' moves on the track, and any changes in their cars while they are practicing and racing. Drivers are responsible for remembering their teams' latest strategies, as well as avoiding accidents and costly mistakes on race day.

Ayrton Senna

Brazilian driver Ayrton Senna (1960-1994) is considered to be one of the best drivers in Formula One history. During his ten-year career, Senna achieved 65 pole positions and won 41 races, as well as three World Championships. On the track, Senna handled his car well and was determined to win. On May 1, 1994, Senna raced in the Grand Prix of San Marino for the Williams-Renault team. Leading the race, Senna lost control of his car and left the track at 193 miles per hour (311 kilometers per hour) and struck a concrete wall. Senna died from his injuries. Three days of national mourning were declared for him in Brazil.

(below) Ayrton Senna with Nigel Mansell (left) and Gerhard Berger (right) after winning the Hungarian Grand Prix.

(bottom) Ayrton Senna raced for Lotus-Renault at the 1985 French Grand Prix.

Alain Prost

French driver Alain Prost (1955-) is considered one of the greatest drivers in Formula One history. Prost earned the nickname "The Professor" because of his ability to think strategically on the track. He is known for beginning races slowly, then speeding to victory at the end. Prost has raced for teams Renault, McLaren-Mercedes, Ferrari, and Williams F1. He has won four World Championships and 51 Grands Prix races, and has achieved 33 pole positions. Prost retired from Formula One racing in 1993.

(right) Alain Prost getting into his car at the Canadian Grand Prix.

(below) Gilles Villeneuve at the Dutch Grand Prix of 1979. The Gilles Villeneuve track in Montreal was named after the driver upon his death. The circuit is now home to the Canadian Grand Prix.

Gilles Villeneuve

Canadian driver Gilles Villeneuve (1952-1982) began his Formula One racing career with the McLaren-Mercedes team in 1977 and joined the Ferrari team in 1978. During qualifying for the 1982 Belgian Grand Prix, Villeneuve was tragically killed in an accident. Villeneuve won six Grand Prix races throughout his short career. His son, Jacques, is also a driver, having raced Indy Cars as well as Formula One. He won the 1997 World Championship for Williams F1.

Michael Schumacher at the 2000 German Grand Prix. He could not finish the race, but went on to match Ayrton Senna's record of 41 first-place finishes later that year.

Michael Schumacher

Michael Schumacher (1969-), from Germany, is one of the best known and highly paid drivers in Formula One racing. Schumacher's Formula One career began in 1991, when he raced in the Belgian Grand Prix. Since 1996, he has been racing for Ferrari, and has won more World Championships than any other driver. At the end of the 2005 season, Schumacher had achieved 64 pole positions in 232 races.

(below) Rubens Barrichello (left) and Michael Schumacher (right) were Ferrari teammates before Barrichello began racing for Honda in 2005.

Rubens Barrichello

Brazilian driver Rubens Barrichello (1972 -) was a very successful driver in his youth. When he was only 19 years old, Barrichello competed in **Formula 3000**, a racing series established by the F.I.A. Barrichello joined the Formula One series in 1993. He was nearly killed in a crash during practice at the San Marino Grand Prix in 1994, just two days before Ayrton Senna's fatal crash. Barrichello raced for the Stewart Grand Prix in 1997, the Ferrari team in 2000, and joined the Honda team in 2005.

Fernando Alonso

Spanish driver Fernando Alonso (1981-) is the youngest driver ever to win the World Championship title. After competing in **kart** competitions, open-wheel races, and Formula 3000, Alonso joined the Minardi team racing in 2001. Since 2002, Alonso has been racing for Renault. He became the youngest driver to win a pole position at the 2003 Malaysian Grand Prix, and the youngest driver to win a Formula One race at the 2003 Hungarian Grand Prix.

(above) Fernando Alonso became Formula One World Champion in 2005, at the age of 24.

Women on Wheels

There have been few female drivers in the history of Formula One. The first woman to compete in Formula One racing was Maria Teresa de Filippis from Italy, who competed in five races from 1958 to 1959. Italian driver Lella Lombardi raced in 17 Grand Prix races in the 1970s, and was the first female driver to finish in the top six. English driver Divina Galica also competed in Formula One races in the 1970s. South African driver Desire Wilson raced in the 1970s and 1980s, then went on to compete in CART and Indy racing, two American open-wheeled racing series. Giovanna Amati from Italy joined the Brabham team in 1992. Many people believe that female drivers have been unsuccessful because of **discrimination**.

Desire Wilson raced Indy cars at the Indy 500, as well as in Formula One.

Behind the Races

Many people are involved in each Grand Prix weekend, aside from the drivers and their teammates. Race marshals, scrutineers, and other track personnel all play important roles on race day.

Race Officials

The race director is responsible for examining cars before each Grand Prix, and also controls the lights at the start of every race. Race marshals communicate track conditions through the use of flags and signs. Scrutineers inspect all cars several times before a race, including weighing the cars and drivers after races to ensure that all teams obey the technical regulations outlined in the F.I.A. rule book.

(below) Bernie Ecclestone (center) became president of the Formula One Constructors Association (FOCA) in 1978. The FOCA represents the racing teams and works with the F.I.A. to make new rules and regulations.

(bottom) A race marshal alerts a driver to track conditions.

Sponsors

It costs millions of dollars for a Formula One team to compete in just one race. Teams are funded by sponsors, which are companies that pay for teams' costs in return for advertising. Sponsors promote their products by advertising on team clothing, drivers' gear, and the cars themselves, as well as on billboards around the track. The logos and names of major sponsors, who provide the team with most of their funding, are placed on the most visible parts of the race car, such as on the front and rear wings, and the engine cover. Smaller sponsors receive smaller areas for advertising on clothing and on less visible parts of the car.

(above) Max Mosley became president of the F.I.A in 1991. The F.I.A. president is one of the final authorities on changes to Formula One rules and regulations.

(right) Fernando Alonso's helmet and jacket are covered with advertising from his team's sponsors. Race teams would not be able to hire the best mechanics and afford the latest equipment without support from their sponsors.

Safety Car

The safety car comes onto the track at critical moments in the race, after a bad accident or another obstacle blocks the track. When the safety car drives onto the track, the other cars lower their speed and form a pack behind it until the track has been cleared. A skilled driver must safely lead the pack around the accident or obstacle. A race official sits in the safety car with the driver and remains in constant contact with race controllers through radios.

Glossary

annual Something that happens once a year

carbon fiber A strong, lightweight material

center of gravity An invisible spot in an object that supports its weight so it does not fall over

cockpit The place where the driver sits

compress To squeeze something

constructor A manufacturer of Formula One cars

cylinder A chamber, or tube, within which a piston, or disk, pumps up and down

dehydration Lacking water or other fluids

discrimination Unfair treatment of someone because of race, sex, or age

drag The force that slows down a car

drivetrain The parts that connect the transmission to the wheel axles in a car

endorsement A promotion for a product or service

Formula 3000 A type of formula open-wheel racing used as a stepping stone for drivers moving on to Formula One

gearbox The device that contains gears in a car

gears The mechanisms that allow a driver to adjust the speed of a car

ignite When a tiny spark causes combustion

jack A device used to raise a car up on one side

kart A racing series that features small four-wheeled vehicles

logo A design that represents a company or organization

manufacturer A company or maker of a product

podium A platform where people stand to receive awards

press conference A period of time reserverd for media questions and photographs

race marshal Someone who ensures that a Grand Prix race runs safely

scrutineer Someone who ensures that teams obey the rule book

sponsorship Money given to a person or team from a company in exchange for promotion of the company's products or services

suspension The system of springs and shock absorbers that help a car handle bumps

turbulence The unsteady movements of a car that are caused by wind whipping around it

Index

32

Printed in the U.S.A.